A PROBLEM SHARED

TALKING ABOUT
DEATH

Louise Spilsbury

PowerKiDS press

New York

Published in 2023 by The Rosen Publishing Group, Inc.
29 East 21st Street, New York, NY 10010

Copyright © 2020 Franklin Watts, a division of Hachette Children's Group

All rights reserved. No part of this book may be reproduced in any form without permission in writing from the publisher, except by a reviewer.

Editor: Amy Pimperton
Designer and illustrator: Collaborate

Cataloging-in-Publication Data

Names: Spilsbury, Louise.
Title: Talking about death / Louise Spilsbury.
Description: New York : Powerkids Press, 2023. | Series: A problem shared | Includes glossary and index.
Identifiers: ISBN 9781725338777 (pbk.) | ISBN 9781725338791 (library bound) | ISBN 9781725338784 (6pack) | ISBN 9781725338807 (ebook)
Subjects: LCSH: Children and death--Juvenile literature. | Death--Juvenile literature. | Death--Psychological aspects--Juvenile literature. | Loss (Psychology)--Juvenile literature. | Bereavement--Juvenile literature. | Grief--Juvenile literature.
Classification: LCC HQ1073.3 S645 2023 | DDC 155.9'37--dc23

Manufactured in the United States of America

CONTENTS

Death and grief	4
Was it my fault?	6
Time to talk	8
I'm scared I might die too!	10
Getting help	12
I'm so angry	14
Letting feelings out	16
I have to be brave	18
Letting go	20
I'm so lonely	22
Opening up	24
Finding help	26
Take your time	28
Glossary	30
Further information	31
Helplines and index	32

DEATH AND GRIEF

At some point in their life, everyone will be affected by the death of someone they care about and the grief that follows.

Many people die because they're very old and their body is worn out. Some people die when their body is damaged by a bad accident or they have had a very serious illness or disease that couldn't be cured.

When someone dies their body stops working and there is nothing anyone can do to stop this, no matter how much we wish otherwise. Coping with the loss of someone you love is one of life's biggest challenges.

Everyone's experience of grief will be different, but may include feeling:
- shocked or numb
- sad
- anxious or scared
- tired and worn out
- guilty and filled with regret
- angry
- calm
- that it's too difficult to concentrate on things, such as schoolwork.

IT'S OK

Don't worry if you swing between feeling fine one minute and upset the next, or that just when everything seems OK, a wave of feelings comes over you. It's perfectly normal to feel a mix of emotions when you're grieving.

SHARING PROBLEMS

Everyone is unique and there's no right or wrong way to grieve, but one thing that most people who are grieving say can help is talking.

"A problem shared is a problem halved," or so the saying goes and it is true that sharing how we feel with someone else usually helps us to deal with those feelings. In this book we meet people who dealt with the difficulties they experienced after a death by sharing the problem and find out what happened when they did.

WAS IT MY FAULT?

When someone dies, their loved ones often feel anger or regret about things they said or didn't have the chance to say. This is totally normal, but such feelings can get worse if people aren't able to talk about them or if they feel guilty about the death. This is Sam's story.

Sam

My grandad died a week ago and I've hardly slept or eaten since then. I feel sad and like I'm such a horrible person. Grandad had been ill for months and Mom was always so busy worrying about him and visiting him that everything felt different at home and we never had fun any more.

One day, I got so angry. I shouted that I wished Grandad would hurry up and die! The next day the hospital called to say he'd died.

Mom has hardly spoken to me since and no one wants me to go to the funeral, even though my big sister Ella is going. I'm so sad about Grandad that I can't sleep or eat, but I can't talk to anyone because it feels as if they all blame me too.

RED FLAG

If someone stops eating and sleeping properly, these are red flags, signals that they are not coping and need help. They may struggle to sleep and eat because they are holding in hurt and worry. It may be up to someone else to encourage them to talk about and share their problem.

WHAT SHOULD SAM DO?

1 Should he get on with things and try to forget his feelings to avoid upsetting his mom?

2 Should he talk to someone about the problem?

3 Should he insist that he goes to the funeral?

TIME TO TALK

Ella, Sam's older sister, stops by his room to complain that he is hiding in there to avoid helping out with chores while their mom is busy sorting out funeral arrangements. Ella explains what happened next.

When I told Sam off for not helping, he yelled at me about how unfair it was that he wasn't going to the funeral. Then he broke down in tears. I had no idea he felt everyone was angry with him for what he said before Grandad died.

I told him that no one blames him and nothing he did or said caused Grandad's death. I feel bad because I didn't visit Grandad the day before he died – I went shopping instead!

Mom didn't want him at the funeral because she thought he was too young, but I said I'd talk to her about letting him come too.

Ella

TALK IT THROUGH

Sam felt much better after talking to Ella and sharing some memories of their grandad. Mom agreed Sam could choose to go to the funeral and explained what it would be like. Together, they decided he would sit with an aunt who could take him out for a break if it all got to be too much.

TOP TIPS

Funerals can be very upsetting and it's important to do what feels right to you. Remember, there are other ways to say goodbye:

- write a goodbye letter to say all the things you didn't get the chance to say
- gather some photos to display at the funeral
- pick a song to be played at the funeral
- place flowers at the grave afterwards (if there is one).

I'M SCARED I MIGHT DIE TOO!

Losing someone you love brings up all sorts of different feelings. As well as guilt, anger, and sadness, death can make people feel scared too. This is Zara's story.

Zara

My best friend Jaz died a month ago. She seemed OK, but then suddenly stopped coming to school. A while later I found out she had been ill and suddenly died.

I saw her parents when I went to the funeral, but I never dared to ask what her illness was and what happened when she died. Was she scared? Did it hurt? My mom said she didn't think we should dwell on what happened. She said we should try to remember Jaz at her best.

But I can't let it go. I hung out with Jaz a lot before she got sick and I lie awake wondering if her illness was catching. I've got no energy and feel weak and I get headaches and stomachaches. I often get a tightness in my chest and sometimes find it hard to breathe. I'm really scared I could die of the same thing Jaz did.

WHAT SHOULD ZARA DO?

1 Try to remember Jaz at her best and forget about the illness?

2 Visit Jaz's parents to ask about what happened?

3 See a doctor to talk about her headaches, chest tightness and health problems?

WHAT DO YOU THINK?

Think about how the different options affect Zara and could affect other people, such as Jaz's parents. Does this help you decide which answer is best?

GETTING HELP

Zara's mom gets worried about Zara's health after she has been complaining about headaches and stomachaches a lot. So she takes Zara to the doctor for a check-up. Dr. Brown explains what happened next.

Dr. Brown

I examined Zara, but soon realized from talking to her that the physical symptoms she is feeling, such as stomachache and a tightness in the chest, are to do with grief. Sometimes our emotions can affect our physical bodies too. Grief over losing her best friend is the most likely cause of her health problems.

As we talked, I also realized Zara was worrying she'd caught Jaz's illness from her. I reassured her that this was unlikely as it was probably a very rare illness. While everyone will die at some time, most people don't die when they are young. Sadly, there are a very few who have serious illnesses or accidents, like Jaz, but most people live until they are very old. Zara is healthy and has no reason to worry.

MAKING A PLAN

Zara was very relieved to hear she wasn't seriously ill. She decided to talk more about her feelings with her mom and explain how worried she has been. She plans to do some things to reduce her anxiety, such as take up soccer training, which she used to love.

TOP TIPS

Doing some sport or other exercise you enjoy is not only a good way to stay fit, it is also a great way to relieve stress — especially if you spend some time outdoors in the fresh air.

I'M SO ANGRY

A sudden death in a family is shattering. There is no chance to say goodbye and no time to prepare for it. The person is just gone from your life. In many cases the cause of a sudden death is violent and shocking too. This is Natalie's story.

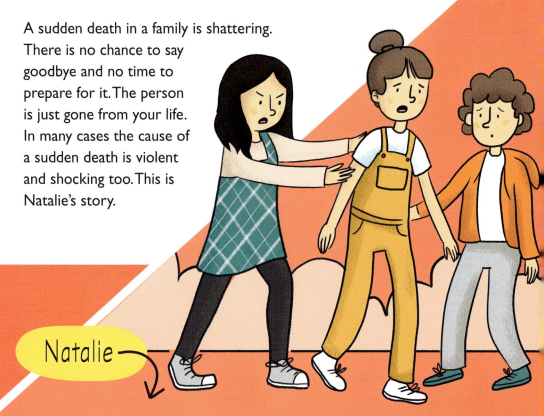

Natalie

My mom died in a car crash. It happened while I was at school and when I came home she wasn't there. I couldn't believe she was gone. I felt numb all over. At first I could barely speak, but it was later I started to feel angry.

Now I feel so angry at everyone and everything. I'm angry with Mom for not being here and with Dad too – he won't talk to me. I'm angry with the doctors for not saving her ... and I'm angry with myself when I laugh at something, because I feel like I'm forgetting her already.

I get into arguments and lose my patients when people complain about homework or annoying parents. Don't they know their problems are nothing compared to mine? One day I got so mad I shoved a girl in my class. I felt a bit mean, but I just don't care about anyone any more.

RED FLAG

If someone suddenly starts shouting and lashing out, this is a red flag or signal that they aren't expressing their emotions in a healthy way. They need to find a better way to safely release those feelings.

WHAT SHOULD NATALIE DO?

1 Talk to someone about her feelings?

2 Find a way to vent her feelings, such as going for a run?

3 Nothing – it's natural to feel angry?

LETTING FEELINGS OUT

Natalie's dad got a call from school saying that while they understand why she is upset, she cannot be allowed to take her anger out on other students. Natalie's dad explains how he responded.

When I first got the call from school, I was angry. I thought ... haven't we had enough to deal with, without Nat getting into scrapes at school?

Then I realized my anger was really about her mom's sudden death, just like Nat's, but unlike Nat I'd been bottling mine up. Nat and I had a good talk. I told her that it is natural to feel angry, but that we both have to find better ways to get our anger out. We decided on an "anger cushion" – a big pillow that we beat up anytime we need to. It helps us to calm down.

I told her that I too felt guilty if I ever had fun or laughed, but that having fun and being happy sometimes is fine and important. It's not a betrayal – it's what Mom would've wanted.

MAKING CHANGES

Natalie and her dad make a plan to be kind to themselves and each other and to make time to talk about Mom, but also to do things they enjoy. Natalie still feels sad a lot and angry sometimes, but now she feels she can handle it better.

TOP TIPS

If there is no anger cushion nearby, try this:
1. breathe in and out deeply four times in a row
2. count slowly to four as you inhale
3. count slowly to eight as you exhale
4. focus on feeling the air move in and out of your body.

I HAVE TO BE BRAVE

A death in the family is so painful that sometimes people try to make it easier for each other by hiding their sadness. Avoiding feelings of grief can help people cope at certain moments, but doing so for too long is a bad thing for most people. This is Carter's story.

Carter

After my sister, Lauren, died, Gran gave me a hug and told me to try not to be too sad because I need to be strong for my dad and stepmom. They look so sick and tired, so I try not to cry. I bottle up my feelings and pretend I'm alright. I find myself not mentioning Lauren at all because it might upset them. It's more important to be brave for them.

I'm also trying really hard to be a better person since Lauren died. Lauren always did really well at school and everyone liked her. She never got told off as much as me. I'll never be as good or clever as Lauren, but I try every day to be more like her. It's hard sometimes and I feel very lonely. I'm not sleeping much but it'll be OK.

RED FLAG

Everyone grieves in different ways and not everyone cries or talks a lot about their lost loved one, but the fact that Carter isn't talking about his sister at all is a red flag that he is hiding his feelings.

The way he is trying to change himself and his behavior is a sign that he is not allowing himself to grieve and is feeling bad about himself too.

LETTING GO

One day, after trying so hard to be strong, Carter is taking the trash out when he drops it and all the garbage falls out. He suddenly collapses in a heap, crying. His stepmom, Arlene, sees everything from the window and brings him inside to talk.

Arlene

I thought Carter was coping with Lauren's death and I guess I've been struggling so much I didn't try to find out how he really was. I feel like I've let him down because he was hiding his feelings to stop us all being sad. We both ended up in tears and in a funny way, it felt good. We both felt better for it.

When he said he was sorry that he would never be as good as Lauren, it broke my heart. I knew he'd been making an effort, but I had no idea he felt like that. I never want him to change and I love him just the way he is — even when he's being sassy — though I don't mind if he goes on being a bit more helpful round the house!

TOP TIPS

Crying can help everyone, so don't worry if you need to cry. Here are some reassuring crying tips:

- think of crying like medicine – it's a way to relieve your body of pressure and stress, and make you feel better
- after you've been crying, have a drink to replace the liquid you've lost and maybe an apple or banana to give you some energy
- sometimes people don't feel like crying, even when they're sad, and that is OK too.

I'M SO LONELY

Feeling really sad is the most normal feeling of all when someone dies. Sadness can also be a very lonely feeling. Grief can make you feel different from other people and that can make it very hard to talk about, which makes you feel lonelier still. This is Cameron's story.

Cameron

After my dad died three months ago I talked to my best friend, Alfie, about it and he was really kind and understanding at first. Dad used to take the two of us to basketball practice and matches, but now it seems Alfie thinks I should be over it. For him life goes on, which seems a bit thoughtless to me.

When I said I didn't feel up to playing basketball with him, he even said I should try to cheer up. He just has no idea what I'm feeling, so now I just keep quiet about it. He looks bored or embarrassed when I say something about Dad anyway, so now I try to push thoughts of Dad to the back of my mind.

The trouble is that the more I do that, the more scared I feel that I'm forgetting Dad and I don't want that. I just feel like I'm in a long black tunnel and things will never get better.

OPENING UP

Cameron decides that he doesn't want to lose Alfie's friendship. He waits until after school when they are walking home alone together to start the conversation.
This is Alfie's side of the story.

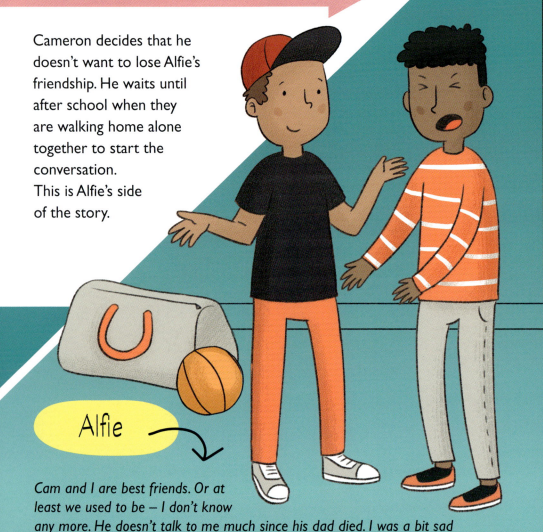

Cam and I are best friends. Or at least we used to be – I don't know any more. He doesn't talk to me much since his dad died. I was a bit sad too, as I knew his dad, but it's been a couple of months now and he seems to not want to do things with me, like coming to basketball practice.

I said he should look on the bright side because he still has his mom, which he does, but he looked so mad that I shut up. I didn't mean it in a bad way – I just want to help him, but I don't know how. I don't talk about his dad because I don't want to upset him, not because I don't care. I was really glad when Cam talked to me about it again.

TALK IT THROUGH

Since Cameron and Alfie talked it through, Alfie tries to just listen and let Cameron talk about his dad. Cameron now plays basketball again, so the friends have some fun together too. But Cameron also realizes he needs to talk to someone who really understands what he's going through, so he asks a teacher for help.

TOP TIPS

Let close friends know how they can help and when you want or don't want to talk about your grief. It can be hard to ask for a shoulder to cry on, but good friends will understand.

FINDING HELP

Cameron's teacher told him that after his wife's death he found a support group – where he could talk to other people in the same situation – really helpful. He asked the school counselor to find Cameron a peer bereavement group that Cameron could join.

Cameron

Finding out how other people felt when someone they loved died and sharing our experiences has definitely helped me to feel better. It's so good to talk to people who understand. I don't feel so alone any more and when I'm at school I'm more patient with friends who don't know what it's like.

Talking helped me realize that playing basketball and being happier doesn't mean I'm forgetting Dad. I will remember him forever. I'm more confident about sharing memories of him with my family too.

Mom and I have started a memory box with pictures and stuff in it about Dad. If we win the basketball tournament next year I'll put the medal in the memory box – it's a way to go on sharing things with Dad, and I like that.

TOP TIPS

Some people find group therapy works. Others prefer to talk one-to-one with a counselor. The key thing is to find someone to talk to who understands and can help you.

NEW IDEAS

Can you think of other ways to keep the memory of someone you love alive? Perhaps by writing about it, drawing pictures, or visiting places they liked, for example?

TAKE YOUR TIME

People sometimes ask how long grief lasts after someone has died. Will things ever get better or will they always feel sad? There are no straight answer to questions like these because grief is different for each person.

Grief changes over time. Gradually, most people find that their feelings of grief aren't there all the time and they have more good days and fewer bad days. Sometimes feelings are stronger than others, for example on special days like a birthday, when they may be caught off guard by a wave of grief that washes over them.

The important thing to remember is that you don't have to go through grief alone. You can talk to friends, family, teachers, doctors, or religious leaders.

All schools should have some form of counseling available to their students, if they need it. There are also bereavement resources and helplines that you can use (see pages 31–32).

LOOKING FORWARD

Everyone comes to terms with death in their own way and in their own time. Over time and with support, people learn to live with their loss and although some days may be tougher than others, they do eventually feel better.

TOP TIPS

Here are some ways to help you cope with grief:
- take care of yourself: eat well, exercise, and try to get a good night's sleep
- spend time doing things you enjoy, like playing a sport, doing a hobby, watching a good film, or playing a computer game
- write about or draw your thoughts, feelings, and memories
- Sometimes you may want to forget. When you want to remember, you could listen to music you enjoyed together and relish those memories.

GLOSSARY

anxious when you feel worried, nervous or scared about something

bereavement a person who is bereaved has had someone close to them who has died

betrayal when a person has done something disloyal or broken a promise

counselor someone who is trained to give advice on personal problems, such as a psychologist or therapist

dwell to keep thinking or talking about a past event – especially an event that is very sad

funeral a ceremony held after a person has died that usually includes their burial or cremation (when a body is burned to ashes)

grief intense sadness, usually caused by the death of someone or something you love

guilty how you feel if you have done something bad or wrong

regret feeling sad about something you did or failed to do

relish to get great enjoyment from something

stress mental or emotional strain or tension caused by difficult events or circumstances

FURTHER INFORMATION

BOOKS

Dorn, Andrea. *When Someone Dies: A Children's Mindful How-To Guide on Grief and Loss.* Eau Claire, WI: PESI Publishing, 2022.

Peden, Seldon. *The Good Mourning: A Kid's Support Guide for Grief and Mourning Death.* Fairfield, IA: 1st World Publishing, 2021.

WEBSITES

When a Loved One Dies: How to Help Your Child
kidshealth.org/en/parents/death.html
This webpage offers advice on how to help children deal with loss and grief.

Somebody in My Friend's Family Died. What Should I Do?
kidshealth.org/en/kids/family-friend-died.html
This webpage discusses the ways people grieve and offers advice on how you can help those who are grieving.

When Somebody Dies
kidshealth.org/en/kids/somedie.html
Read more about coping with death at this website.

HELPLINES

BetterHelp
This online resource makes it easy to find the right therapist for you. Includes a monthly fee when paired with a professional therapist.
www.betterhelp.com

Crisis Text Line
This resource can connect people with a crisis counselor at any time via text messaging. Visit the website to learn how.
www.crisistextline.org

National Suicide Prevention Lifeline
Anyone can call this helpline at any time if they are experiencing suicidal thoughts.
1-800-273-TALK (1-800-273-8255)
suicidepreventionlifeline.org

INDEX

accidents 4, 12
anger 4, 6, 10, 14–15, 16–17
anxiety 13

bereavement group 26

counselors 26, 27
crying 20, 21

doctors 11, 12, 14, 28

eating 6, 7, 29
exercise 13, 29

family 14, 18, 26, 28
feelings 4, 5, 6, 7, 10, 13, 15, 16, 18, 19, 20, 23, 28, 29
flowers 9

friends 20–23, 28
funerals 6, 7, 8, 9, 10

grandparents 6, 8, 9
graves 9
guilt 4, 6, 10, 16

illness 4, 10, 11, 12

letters 9

memories 9, 26, 27, 29

old age 4

regret 4, 6
religious leaders 28

sadness 4, 6, 10, 17, 18, 20, 21, 22, 24, 28

school 4, 10, 14, 16, 18, 24, 26, 28
siblings 8, 9, 18, 19
sleeping 6, 7, 18, 29

talking 5, 9, 12, 19, 26
teachers 25, 26, 28